To Dr. Audrey [illegible]

Our Father

Imprints That Shape Our Lives

Dr. Rosalyn V. Green

Thank you for your encouragement, support, and love. Blessings and Favor!

Dr. "G"

VANTAGE PRESS
New York

FIRST EDITION

Published by Vantage Press, Inc.
419 Park Ave. South, New York, NY 10016

Manufactured in the United States of America
ISBN: 978-0-533-15920-8

Library of Congress Catalog Card No.: 2007907565

0 9 8 7 6 5 4 3 2 1

Foreword

The church of the Living God is in an interesting place in its salvation history. In the midst of a tremendous cry for help from outside our stained glass windows and doors, when we look within we see a growing number of Christians who are hurting in silence and living in ambivalence. Due to this internal conflict, and as a Pastor who has witnessed so many hurting people, the time is now for a word of hope that merges the psychological and the wisdom of God.

I met Dr. Rosalyn V. Green over fifteen years ago and one of my earliest recollections was a conversation we had about how the church shies away from and sometimes even denies that the human psyche is intricately interwoven with the spirit man. Yet our spiritual growth is dependent on how well we handle and resolve the issues of the mind. Being that women are the predominant churchgoers and nurturers of relationships, when they're sick because of unresolved issues, the whole house is sick, including the church house and the family. In this small but powerful book, Dr. Green addresses how women of all ages are impacted by the relationship they have had with or without a father. Although this book specifically addresses women, I encourage both women and men to read and embrace the central message that comes through loud and clear: a healthy relationship with "our father," both physically and spiritually, is essential to living, loving, and thriving in this life.

—Donnie McClurkin, Pastor
Perfecting Faith Church
Freeport, New York

Introduction

Fathers play a critical role in nurturing their children.

The quality of a father's relationship with his daughter is a key factor in determining who she becomes and whom she selects as a mate in her life journey. The bond between father and daughter helps to shape a woman's future as she moves ahead with her career and male relationships. According to founder and director of Just For Us Workshops, Carole Isenberg, "Women who have supportive fathers reach a higher level of achievement and are better equipped to choose good mates." Fathers have a two-part role, one role as a parent and the other role as a paradigm for all men.

So consider this is one of the most influential persons in the life of his daughter, whether either realizes it or not. Not only does this relationship lay the foundation for a girl's attitude toward relationships, and marriage, it also lays the foundation for her relationship with God. Girls who are secure in their femininity generally have fathers who encourage them to reach their fullest potential in all areas of their lives. The opposite is also true for daughters who have no relationships or poor relationships with their fathers.

Daughters need love and affirmation from their fathers as well as their mothers. It is believed that a girl's first "male love" is her father and thus he becomes the first prototype of her relationship with men. How Dad responds to his "little girl" and how he encourages her to respond to him will help to form the basis for how she will respond to men in general with whom she relates. With a sharp sense of intuition, a girl will form an opinion of herself and women in general by observing how her father treats her mother and other women. If daddy treats the women in his life with respect, then she will learn that women are to be respected and she will expect and demand to be treated so. Her future relationships with men usually mirror the type of relationship she had with her father. The absent father or having not receiving the appropriate fatherly attention in the early stages of her life, leaves the girl searching for love and affirmation in other relationships and from other sources. Detrimental consequences can happen to her if she attempts to fulfill those unmet needs in destructive behaviors and/or relationships. When a father is, or has been, absent—emotionally or physically, and abusive (emotionally/physically/sexually)—the girl feels the emptiness, pain, anger, rejection, and abandonment.

> For girls whose fathers are not involved, many positive character and personality traits fail to be developed. Girls deprived of strong relationships with their fathers tend to grow up with the perception that men are irresponsible and untrustworthy. As adolescents they commonly become obsessed with heterosexual relationships. In a desperate search for substitute forms of male affection, some have inappropriate sexual contacts, become overly dependent on men, and allow men to take advantage of them. (David Popence, *Life Without Father*: Compelling new evidence that fatherhood and marriage are indispensable for the good of children and society. p. 159.)

Promiscuity and pregnancy are often classic outcomes of "fatherless" daughters—as they seek their identity in relation to men and need attention and love from the male sex. According to Jelani Mandara, Assistant Professor of Human Development and Social Policy, this early acting out of "fatherless" girls is not always immediate in African-American families. The effect on daughters is often seen later in life. He states, "Fathers influence daughters' later relationships with other men." Knowing how to relate to men can be challenging for women who have never really interacted with their fathers. Having a connection with a loving father provides the daughter with the basic resources to navigate through her relationship with other men. Daddy, quite often, becomes the reference point for what a man should be in a woman's life. Girls look at their daddies to determine what men are like, how they act, look, and talk. By watching their fathers, they decide what fathers are like and how men should treat women.

As a grown woman, and probably one of the most beautiful and adored women of her time, Marilyn Monroe regretted that as a little girl no one told her she was pretty. She spent much of her life trying to find the unconditional love and acceptance she longed for as a little girl. Marilyn Monroe led a lonely life of self-doubt and loathing, had numerous affairs, and three marriages to much older men. The task of validating a little girl's femininity is one of the most important roles of the most significant man in her life: her father.

Our relationship with our dad was and is the springboard for our selection of the man or men in our life. We first learned about a man and woman's relationship from our mommies and our daddies, or the significant males/females that we grew up with, even if one was not physically there. We observed their behavior and interaction between each other and then placed our own interpretation to that information. We furtively gathered all of the necessary inner and outerwear soul and heart clothing and packed them into our trunk for our lifelong journey. The issue is we have either overpacked too much of everything, or we didn't pack the right articles of clothing to wear. I think you might need to consider another analogy here. Consequently, we are uncomfortable with what we are wearing, but don't know quite what to do with what we are carrying in our trunk because, we are too far away from home too go back, it's too expensive to buy all new clothes, we don't want to get rid of some things because, they are "just so nice," even though we can't wear them anymore, and we go on and on rationalizing why we continue to drag our luggage.

Many women who experienced a dysfunctional, distant or nonexistent relationship with their fathers as children have suffered in their adult relationships.

Our Father

One

I always wanted to be Daddy's Little Girl. You know, when he walked in the door, his face lit up and he reached for me and tossed me up in the air and then when I came down, I was in the center of his arms and he gave me the biggest hug and kiss on the cheek. Daddy would look at me in my eyes and say, "I love you and you are my sweetheart!" Didn't all of us girls want that from our dads? But, for the most part, that is not what we got. Instead we got the dad that came in from work beat down from the job and outside world who was usually almost too tired to lift his feet, much less lift us up. Although we kept wishing that he would acknowledge his girls in some special way as we sat quietly in the room, trying to gauge his mood, and decide if we should go to him since he hadn't come to us, he never came. And we're still trying to decipher our man's mood and decide how we should approach him.

When I looked up from my crib while I was crying, I saw this man who seemed to always be around somewhere. He picked me up and rocked me in his arms and softly whispered to me that everything was going to be all right. He asked me did I need changing, was I hungry, what was wrong? Right then I began to realize that this man was someone whom I could begin to trust. This was possibly someone who cared about me. I didn't know he was my daddy until he told me—I'm your daddy, say Da Da.

Did that really happen or was that something that I so

desperately wanted that I simply made it up? Maybe the story actually went like this:

I didnt't know what was going on but I knew that something was hurting me and I was crying. First, just a small whimper, and then a little louder. No one came. Maybe they couldn't hear me. So, I began to scream, still nothing. Now I am so tired from crying, I am back to a whimper in between my sighs and hiccups. I began to realize no one was coming. I was on my own. Wait, I do hear someone coming. But it's the lady who says she's my mother but she always seems angry with me. What did I do to make her so mad at me? I am afraid, because I know she's going to start yelling at me and telling me about my "no good daddy." She might even hit me. I wish "no good daddy" was here. Maybe he could help me. He probably won't come—I have been wishing for him to come and get me for a long time. I probably wouldn't like him either because he'll just yell at me too. I have to learn to stand up for myself, because I don't have anybody but me.

Guess what? He came! Daddy finally came! He's finally here. I'm a little bit older, but I can still be daddy's little girl. He does tell me "I'm your daddy and you're daddy's sweetheart and you're to do everything that daddy tells you to do." I am so excited and so happy. I'm going to be the best little girl and I'm going to be so good, he's going to love me forever and never leave me again. But daddy is touching me and mommy told me not to let anyone touch me in my private places. Maybe this is okay because this is daddy and I am supposed to do everything that he tells me to do. I don't know. This doesn't feel right. This hurts. This hurts a lot. Should I tell mommy, will she yell at me, will she believe me, will she make him stop, will he leave me again? What do I do? Daddy does love me. Every time he comes to my room, he tells me so. He told me not to tell mommy about our special visits because this was his special love for me. I am so confused about my daddy—I love him but I don't want him to do those things to me. They make me feel different. Sometimes he makes me feel good, sometimes bad, sometimes I don't feel anything. I just pretend he's not there. I don't know about being Daddy's Little Girl.

Two

When I cried this time, daddy was there, but he was yelling at mommy and me. I thought this time might be like the last time when he came and got me and smiled at me. Well, I don't know what he's going to be at any given time. Every other week daddy comes home, yells at mommy and me and then hits mommy. I run and hide, but I can still hear her crying. When I grow up, is he going to do the same thing to me? I am going to be so good and quiet as a mouse so that he won't get me.

As I grew up, I realized that daddy only acted mean when he drank or when he smoked those funny smelling cigarettes. I learned how to be invisible when he got like that. I had a lot of feelings about a lot of things, but I stuffed them all down inside of me. I tried to take care of him and mommy so that we could all be a happy family. I got straight "A's" in school. They would never have to worry about me.

Three

My daddy was the first man to tell me how pretty I was and how I was his little princess. When he tossed me in the air, I just giggled and giggled because, although he acted as though he was going to drop me, I knew he would never drop me and he never did. I trusted him. Mommy would try to make him stop, but he would just laugh and give her a kiss and keep right on playing with me. When I got sick, mommy would take care of me while daddy was at work, but she would tell me that daddy would come in and see me as soon as he got home.

When daddy got home he came to my bedroom and kissed me on the forehead and asked me what was wrong with daddy's baby. He would sit on the bed and hold my hand and read a book to me until I fell asleep. He was my comforter. When I thought the boogey man was hiding in my room, under my bed or in my closet, daddy came in my room and scared him away. Daddy was my protector.

My very first date was with my daddy. One day he came home early from work to take me out to lunch. Mommy helped me to pick out my prettiest dress and daddy had on a suit. I even got to pick the restaurant. I was special. Of course I knew mommy was special, too, because they went out together and I had to stay home with the babysitter. I guess that was all right because I got to have my time with daddy all by myself too.

Four

Daddy's little girl is all grown up now. If I have a good perception of daddy, I feel good about myself, because you see, when I was growing up, I gained my self-image through the eyes of others. Because I have no knowledge of me, the only way I can learn about me is from the most significant people who are raising me and parenting me. These persons may or may not have been my parents, but whoever they were, they impacted me. I watched how mommy and daddy interacted with each other, how they talked to each other. Little did they know about how much they were teaching me or the messages they were giving me.

I'm 46. As I sit here in my therapist's office with my third husband, I am in so much pain emotionally and mentally that I can only groan as she asks me questions about my childhood. My therapist is asking me to tell her about my relationship with my father. I put my hand over my mouth to hold back from screaming gutturally. Tears are streaming down my face and I begin rocking back and forth because I want to run out of there. My therapist takes my baby, my sixth child, from my husband and he moves closer to me and begins to hug me. She moves closer to me, while rocking the baby, and calmly touches my hand and encourages me to talk about what is giving me so much pain. I am so afraid about what is going to happen to me if I open up and begin to tell how I really feel. Slowly, between groans, I began to tell her how my mother died when I was five years old. I didn't know and still don't know why she died. I suspect that she was terminally ill, but we were never told anything. All I know is that my mother left me. Just before my mother died, my father gave us to his mother, our grandmother to raise us. I guess he felt as though he couldn't care for us and a dying wife also. So, he left us. I was so bewildered. What was happening to our family?

When we got to our grandmother, she seemed very old to me and very cranky. There were six of us kids and she probably didn't want to take care of all of us, but she had to. While living with my grandmother, it seemed as though she hated me. I was always the one that got into trouble at home and at school. I was always being whipped and/or punished for something I did or didn't do. I wasn't as pretty as my other three sisters. They had fairer skin than mine and their hair was also longer and easier to comb. I had short thick hair, which was hard to get even a straightening comb through, and I was the darkest one in my family. I was told I was mean and I acted mean.

I learned to be hard and tough. No one was going to hurt me or leave me again. So when the therapist asked me to tell her about my childhood and my relationship with my father and my brothers, all I could think about was the pain I felt then and still feel now. I thought about all the times I had been teased and taunted by my brothers and his friends. I thought about how I had been laughed and snickered at in school not only by the boys, but also by the girls.

I remember daddy coming to see us at grandma's house but having very little to say to me. It seemed as though everyone was happy with everyone else except me. I felt as though no one liked me, not even daddy.

Five

My husband and I were in therapy because we just couldn't get along. We couldn't talk to each other. Every time we opened our mouths to each other we ended up fighting. The therapist asked us did we want our marriage? We looked at each other and rolled our eyes. This was prior to her asking me about my life. Now here I sit, crying and in such pain and she's asking me to talk to her. I look at my therapist hesitantly, because I'm afraid I'm going to see that she won't like me either. But as she holds my baby and holds my hand, all I see and feel is love and empathy from her, as if she actually can feel my pain. My husband has his arm around me and he's rubbing my shoulder and she's holding my hand. Maybe I can trust them and finally let go of all the hurt and talk to them. Although, I don't believe that my husband really loves me because he did leave me twice before.

The therapist encourages me to talk and I begin to share my growing up days. She looks at me with such compassion in her eyes that I turn away. People don't look at me with love, they're always angry. I don't know how to deal with someone who shows me love, thus when I talk with people I tend to look down. She softly speaks to me and tells me to look at her, and then she tells me that she sees and feels my pain. She also tells me that beyond all of my gruffness she sees sweetness in me. I look at her in disbelief. How could she know that deep down inside I really am and want to be a very sweet and loving person? I just don't know how to bring that part of me out.

I begin to cry even harder. The therapist coaxes me to look at her again and she asks me to tell her what I really want from my husband. I brokenly respond that I want my husband to love me and not leave me again.

Six

Well, here I am at my girlfriend's house. I've just left my husband of twenty-five years. I couldn't do it anymore. I knew he was bisexual when I married him at eighteen, but I was sure that he would change over time. You see I was going to be the one woman that made the difference in his life. Because of my love for him and my loving to him, he had to go straight. At least that's what I thought. Where did I go wrong?

Growing up I had been sexually abused by my father; at least I thought he was my father. I found out when I was twenty that my dad was not really my daddy. My real daddy was the preacher in my church. So, daddy was my stepfather. Was that why he messed with me? He was also an alcoholic. Mama made me go to church and be nice to the preacher and my stepfather, even though she knew that they were touching me and doing things to me. Why did she consistently make me be around them? I decided that when I grew up I was going to control everything and no one was going to ever hurt me again. Could that be the reason I married a gay man, well, a bisexual man? But he was so good to me and he was fifteen years older than I was. Maybe I was searching for my "daddy."

I thought our marriage was pretty good. I was a good housekeeper and took excellent care of our three children. From the outside it looked as if we had the perfect marriage. We lived in a beautiful home in an upscale neighborhood, attended a large progressive church, sang in three choirs, and sent our children to private school. Yet, he continued to go out and stay away from the kids and me for days at a time. I knew where he was and sometimes, I even went over there to make him come home. I noticed men, both young and old, always surrounded him, but I told myself that they were just his friends. I could not accept that my husband was possibly involved with these men. If I accepted that then, I also had to accept that somehow I had failed. I had not made him change. When introducing my husband to my girlfriends, they were always very polite, but they always seemed to look a little surprised. They knew he was "gay." In hindsight, after leaving him, I was able to look at my husband more objectively. Of course he was "gay." He acted, dressed, talked, and walked effeminately.

One incident that happened very early in our marriage should have given me the insight to what was going on, but I missed it until thirty years later. I was pregnant with our first child and was due at any moment. I remember walking back to my job after my lunch break when the first pains began to hit me. At first I could not move, than slowly, after I got my breath back, I leaned up against a building wall. As I was leaning there, trying to decide what to do, a young man, between the ages of eighteen and twenty, asked me if I was all right. I explained to him what was happening and he so graciously offered to assist me. He enlisted the aid of a policeman and with both of their help, I was rushed to the nearest hospital. The young man stayed with me until my husband came. They met and my husband thanked him profusively for being there for me and with me. Because we were in the South, it was natural for people to help others when in need. As a result of this man's caring nature, we became best friends. He also became very good friends with my husband. Little did I know that after meeting my husband that same night, they became lovers. I found this out thirty some years later. My best male friend was also my husband's main squeeze. Upon finding out this information, that was the straw that broke my back. I couldn't do this anymore. I left the marriage. So, here I am in at my girlfriend's house, with my three children, completely alone for the first time in my life.

I had been determined to make my marriage work and control my life. My thought was that if I had something that I had chosen for me, then I could control everything around me including my husband and my marriage. I was devastated at the demise of not only my marriage, but also the loss of a great friendship with someone of the opposite sex. So what did I do, I retaliated. I decided that I was going to find out what was so special about my best male friend who just happened to be my husband's lover. In my mind I was going to get them both for what they had done to me.

I told my best friend that I knew he was my husband's lover and I played on his guilt of hurting me. I then manipulated him into falling in love with me. So, I could now taunt my husband with the knowledge that not only had he had my best male friend, but that he didn't really have his heart, because, although he was sleeping with my husband, he was in love with me. Oh, how smug I was. I expected that to make me feel better. I had gotten my revenge. But, as I walked away, I felt more confused and worse than I had ever felt in my entire life. Because now my best male friend thought I was going to marry him, now that I was no longer with my husband.

Maybe that was his way of trying to get back at my husband. After trying to work things out myself, one of my closest female friends encouraged to me to seek some counseling.

Seven

I grew up with both parents in the home. They were both Christians, they were even preachers. I loved my mother and father, but for some reason, I could not get along with my father. We clashed at every turn. In my mind, I had an image of how a father was supposed to be and act, and he did not fit the bill. Consequently, I was asking for something from my dad that he was not able to give, although I did not realize this until I was an adult and going through therapy.

My daddy was a very strong man and appeared to be real rough and tough. I wanted affection, hugs and kisses. What I got was rules, structure, and discipline. As I was growing up, I resented him for not giving me what I needed and because of this resentment, I rebelled against him. Thus, we fought constantly. Not getting the expressed love from my father that I needed as a child led me into relationships with men, as an adult, that were unhealthy for me. These relationships were with married men or men who were already involved with other women. I felt as though I was wearing a sign that said, "Married Men Only."

I often asked myself during this period of time why was it that the only men that were attracted to me were either married or involved with someone else. I was unaware that what I was searching for was a reflection of my unfulfilled needs that began as a child. I wanted love, affection, financial security, and self-security from the man I wanted in my life. A single man certainly couldn't meet those stated needs, at least, not the ones I knew. So, what I was looking for came in the older man and most of them were married. I thought it was them, but it was me who was drawing them into my circle. Of course at the time I was unaware of what I was doing, all I knew was that I wanted a man to love me, just me, to be the apple of his eye.

Eight

I was daddy's little girl. He called me his "little cream puff." We did everything together. Daddy was a college professor, so I was home schooled. We had the best relationship a daughter could want. So, what went wrong in my marriage? I have been married for thirty-four years or should I say we have been legally together for thirty-four years, because for the last twenty years we have cohabitated almost as if we were brother and sister. I thought I had married the man of my dreams. I was twenty and he was thirty-five. Even though he was much older than I was, I was a junior in college and he was a doctor, he pursued me relentlessly. I was thrilled, overwhelmed, and in awe of him. After a whirlwind six months courtship, I said yes to his proposal of marriage.

I had no idea that I was his "little girl" and I was not supposed to grow up. Although I did know that I was his second wife, I found out after ten years of marriage that I was not the second but the fourth wife. Well, at this point I was a little concerned, but I figured I could handle it. Entering my early thirties and after fifteen years of marriage, I wanted to have a say in some of the decision-making issues that affected the children and me. To my surprise, I was sort of patted on the head and told I was not to worry my pretty little head about anything, that he would take care of everything. Well, that was no longer good enough for me.

Being thirty-five and becoming assertive, I decided to take matters into my own hands and I made a decision to have my own means economically, in case anything happened. I didn't know what could possibly happen, because at that time it seemed as if we had the perfect marriage. Even with all that, I still had this funny little feeling that I needed to have my own money.

Becoming financially independent of my husband began the demise of my marriage. My husband never forgave me or accepted me for growing up. He decided he would make me pay for changing the rules of the household. He did this by treating me worse than an animal. I was no longer permitted to talk to him and when I did, he simply ignored me completely. He did not speak me to and he did not ask for my opinion of anything. I was treated as if I was a stranger in my own home. I had to pay half of all expenses incurred within the household, and all of the children's expenses. When we went out or traveled together, I had to pay for all of my expenses. I might as well have been single. Our sex life was almost nonexistent; only when he wanted me were we sexually intimate. I could not ask or touch him for fulfillment of my needs and if I did, he would ignore me or blatantly tell me no. Oh, yes, in public, we still acted as if we were the perfect couple.

Did I really grow up, if so, then why I am still in this charade of a marriage? Am I still trying to be my husband's or daddy's little girl?

Nine

I am a beautiful woman, physically. I am part Indian, Japanese, and African-American. I am a strong woman. I grew up without my father being in my life because he was a serviceman and was not around much so I took care of mom and my three brothers. I, also, went to college and graduated with honors and became a very successful attorney. I got married, had a son, stayed in the marriage for twenty years, then decided that I wanted out. Not only did I want out of the marriage, but I also wanted out of all relationships with men. I wanted a same sex relationship. Both my husband and son were horrified.

I need to share some history on why I felt that I was now a lesbian. I was extremely angry and very confused.

Although I was quite successful in my chosen occupation, my personal life was a mess. I wouldn't let my husband know it, but everything he did and said irritated me to no end and made me angry. I was so angry that one day after leaving work, I decided to end it all by taking my life. All I ended up doing was totaling my Mercedes; I walked away without a scratch. I then decided to leave my husband and move in with a woman who seemed to be very interested in me. So, I separated from my husband, leaving my son with him and moved in with this woman.

Things went well for a while, until I became too possessive of her and she decided she needed to move on without me. I was distraught, even frantic. What could I do to make her stay? She could not leave me. I would not let her. Once again I resorted to suicide, but it was going to be in her bedroom, in her bed. When she got home she was going to find me dead in her bed. That would fix her. After slashing my wrists and just before losing consciousness, I dialed my mother's number and told her good-bye. She immediately realized that something was wrong and sent an ambulance to the address where I was. Evidently, it was not meant for me to die.

I was in the hospital on the psychiatric ward for three months. Upon my release, I was advised to see a therapist for ongoing treatment. I went but didn't want to go. She did everything to try to get me to talk but I was adamant in my stance of refusal to talk. I didn't need her to help me. I didn't need anyone. After about three years of talking about surface issues only and sometimes not talking at all, she asked me a very important question, one that she had asked me several times before, and I had adamantly answered no to, because I had suppressed the memories. My therapist asked me if I had ever been sexually abused or molested as a child. For some reason memories began to flood my brain and I began to spill everything.

My male cousin who was babysitting me had sexually abused me at five years old. I remember telling my mother, but she just looked at me and didn't say or do anything. At twelve, my best friend's father, at a sleepover in her home, raped me. I became pregnant as a result of that rape and my mother made me get an abortion. I never told anyone who the father was. They wouldn't believe me anyway. I hate men.

My mother's solution to everything was for me to get married and forget about everything that had happened to me as a child and adolescent. And I almost did, but somewhere along the line while sitting on my therapist's couch, I remembered everything. I am so confused, what do I really want in a relationship? Was I gay? I have mixed feelings about my sexual identity. What am I?

Ten

I had to see someone after having my twins because my postpartum depression was taking over me. I could hardly get out of bed in the mornings, much less take care of a husband, fraternal twins, a boy and a girl who were two years old, and a five-year-old. It was too much. I couldn't do it any longer. Not only did I have still have postpartum depression after two years, I was no longer sexually active with my husband and hadn't been since before the twins were born. As I matter of fact, I could only sleep without being afraid if I slept in the futon in our bedroom. The futon had sides, thus I felt safe. My husband was ready to leave me. I was also having flashbacks or hallucinations every time I looked out my bedroom windows into the wooded area of my yard. I saw glimpses of myself running through the woods, being chased by someone.

Along with wanting no type of intimacy with my husband, I had secretly begun minor self-mutilation. I would go into the bathroom where no one could see me, lock the door, sit on the floor, and take a knife and calmly cut myself very lightly on my arms. Something was drastically wrong, but I didn't know what it was or how to fix it. As I began to relax and open up in therapy I began to share information of how growing up as an Army brat was for me. My father was a very strict colonel in the service and he was also very strict at home. His expectations were for persons under his command to follow through on what was told and expected of them without feedback. My mother was passive and did exactly as he instructed. I never remember her questioning any of his decisions. I questioned many of his plans, decisions, and ideas, but only in my mind. I was an only child so I had no one else to voice my thoughts.

One thing that distinctly reverberates through my early memories of my childhood that related to men was that whenever we visited my paternal grandfather I was never allowed to stay in the house with my grandfather alone. I was not permitted to sleep there either. I remember my parents would stay there and I would visit during the day, but when evening time came, I had to go down the street where my father's sister lived and I had to remain there. My mother would bring me my dinner and snacks, but under no circumstances was I allowed to stay in my grandparents' home. Whenever I questioned them about this arrangement, they would inform me that that was what they wanted and I was instructed not to ask any more questions about it. So, although perplexed, I did as I was told and accepted the status quo. Once I became older, I would only visit during the day and stayed with friends at night. So, what did it matter, so I thought? Later in life, I did find out that what my parents made me do had an impact on me.

I thought about those years as I sat on my therapist's couch. After relating to my therapist's feelings of fear, needing to feel safe when I slept, feeling guilty and wanting to hurt myself, and feeling afraid whenever my husband came close to me or tried to show me any signs of intimacy, she asked me if I could remember being sexually assaulted, hurt, or molested? I emphatically told her that nothing of that nature had ever happened to me. My therapist then asked me about my relationship with my father. I told her that I guessed that it was like any other relationship between fathers and daughters. We were not close, but we got along okay. It was no big deal. When asked about my relationship with my mother, I gave almost the same answer. We got along okay. We weren't lovey dovey. It was just all right. She then asked me about my relationship with my husband and I gave the same answer. After reflecting back on what I had given her, the therapist asked me who was I close to? It was at that precise moment that I realized that I was not close to anyone, not even my husband. Here I was forty years old and really didn't feel as though I had a friend that I could trust or openly talk to.

As the sessions continued, I began to look at my life unraveled before me. Somewhere early in life, I had lost parts of me and I trusted no one. What had happened to me? I wanted to find out, but I was also very afraid of finding out. My therapist never pressured me into excavating deeper into the hidden recesses of my mind, but she gently chipped away at tiny pieces until we got to the real issues. I recall her asking me what was it specifically about my husband that frightened me, and had I always been afraid of my husband. I informed her that I had not always been afraid of him and that I really had no reason to be afraid of him now. My husband had never hit me and seldom raised his voice. He was very supportive of me and encouraged me to do what was important to me. For example, my husband encouraged and supported me in completing school and getting my degree so that I could open my own child care center. I was also an artist and tended to paint whenever I wanted to get away from everyone and everything. My husband also encouraged me in my painting. So why was I so afraid of this man?

My therapist asked me would I be willing to bring in some of my paintings to show her and I said yes. I did not know that she wanted to see if she could interpret those paintings to see if she could get some kind of insight as to what was really going on with me. After viewing the paintings, which were very vivid and bold, my therapist asked me if I could go back in my mind to the times when I was painting them and tell her what I was feeling at the time. As I began to go down memory lane, all I could recall were feelings of rage and anger. I even began to feel angry in the session just thinking about those times. She also asked me if I could remember what prompted me to paint each picture or what had been going on prior to the painting of each picture. We began to realize that there was a pattern. Each painting had occurred after my husband and I had been sexually intimate or after he had tried to be sexually intimate with me and I had refused him. My therapist once again asked me if I had been sexually abused and I replied no, but I wasn't so sure now. All indications looked as if something had happened to me, but I didn't know what it was. It did appear as though whatever had happened was related to men. Exploring a little deeper at each therapeutic session helped me to understand that no matter what had happened to me as a child, I was not to blame.

After approximately two years of therapy, one hour weekly, we had a breakthrough. By now, my husband and I were having marriage counseling to try and put our relationship back on track. To be more specific, the purpose of our therapy was to try to get me, with his help, to accept him intimately and sexually.

I recall sitting in the session and suddenly becoming very afraid after my husband shouted that he didn't know why I wouldn't allow him to touch me. We weren't even sleeping in the same bed any longer. I was sleeping on the futon in our bedroom while he slept in the bed. He stated in a very loud voice that he had never done anything to hurt me. Why was he being blamed for something that he didn't know anything about and it seemed as if his wife didn't know either? I remember, with fists clenched and tears streaming down his cheeks, he jumped up to leave the session. The therapists immediately got up also and put her hands on his shoulder and implored him to stay. She was sure that we were on the edge of a breakthrough and begged my husband to stay so that we could work through the issues and get to the root of our problems. He agreed to try and sat back down beside me.

In my mind I was seeing myself running through the woods and a boy chasing me. I saw myself as a little girl, running and screaming for someone to help me. I became so frightened in the therapy session that I began moaning and crying and went into a fetal position with my arms wrapped around me to ward off the pain. At this point my therapist asked me if she could touch me and I nodded yes. She gently began rubbing my hands while she softly began talking to me, telling me that it was alright, that there was no one there that was going to hurt me. She also asked me if it would be all right for my husband to rub my shoulders. I once again nodded yes to her. As my therapist continued talking to me and rubbing my hands and my husband continued to rub my shoulders, I began to feel my muscles become more relaxed and those frightening tentacles of fear began to slowly leave my body.

Checking to see that I was all right, my therapist then asked me if I could share what had happened to me during the session. I told her that I remembered being sexually molested at four years old by the sixteen-year-old boy who lived next door. I had been told repeatedly by my parents not to go with strangers, and not to go in anyone's house unless they were with me. But I remember being so lonely on that day and not having anyone to play with me. So when my next door neighbor asked me if I wanted to come over there and play some of his video games, I thought it would be okay. I did hesitate a little at first, but then we as a family had been over there with his family so surely this would be okay. So, I went. In the beginning, we did play video games. Then he invited me into his room. Once I got inside, he locked the door. I got scared then, but he wouldn't let me go. I remember him putting me on the bed and pulling down my pants. By now I was crying, but no one could hear me but him. He hurt me because he was so much bigger than me. After it was over, while he lay on the bed breathing hard, I jumped up, unlocked the door and went running into the woods behind our house. Once he realized I was gone, he came running behind me. I got away, but I never told anyone. I was afraid because I had disobeyed my parents' rule. So, I was to blame for what had happened to me.

My therapist helped me to see that I was not the person to be blamed if blame was to be cast upon anyone. She also helped me to see how I was hurting my husband and myself by carrying this weight of abuse. I wondered why I was remembering this at this particular time in my life. My therapist and I concluded that I probably had an unconscious fear of this happening to my daughter who would be turning four in three months. We also discovered that my husband had been sexually abused by his father when he was a child. That was the probable cause of them not allowing me to be alone in the house with my grandfather as I was growing up. Once the pieces of the puzzle began to fit, I then began the healing process.

Eleven

My husband and I have just had the worst fight. My face is swollen, my lip is split, and I have a black eye. My husband is sitting on the side of the bed crying and begging my forgiveness for beating me. He says he doesn't know what makes him go crazy like that, but it will never happen again. Then, he does something that he has never ever done before. He calls a counseling center to set up an appointment for us to see a therapist that day. We are lucky that she can see us immediately. I cringe because the therapist is going to see the physical damage that my husband did to my face. No one has ever seen what he's done to me before, because I've always been able to hide the marks or stay in until they fade away. Well, I don't care anymore; she'll just have to see what he did. I do put on sunglasses and wear them to the session.

The first thing the therapist does after she welcomes us and tells us a little bit about therapy, is to insure my safety in the home. I can press charges and/or go to a shelter. I choose to do none of those things. I was so moved by my husband taking the initiative to seek counseling for us and following through, that I was sure that we could work through any difficulties that we had. The therapist did ask me to remove my sunglasses and I did so, reluctantly. She looked at me, made some notations in her chart, and asked me if I thought I needed to see a medical doctor. I informed her that I didn't. I thought she would then ask me why I would stay with a man that would beat me, but she didn't. She asked us to tell her what precipitated the fight or what was going on prior to our fighting.

We thought for a moment, but we really couldn't remember what had been so monumental that we were beating on each other. It seemed as though that was the way we had existed for the last couple of years.

The therapist then asked us if we could share with her what seemed to make us so angry towards each other. I didn't know where to start. It seemed as though everything my husband did or said made me angry. My husband said he got angry all the time because I was always trying to change him. I explained to the therapist that I wasn't trying to change him, but that he wasn't using all of his skills to his greatest potential. As his wife, I saw my role as helping him to be the best that he could be.

It frustrated me to no end to have to get up every morning and work three jobs, while he lay in the bed. My husband was on disability, after being injured on a job and hurting his back. He was a contractor by trade. I really loved my husband, but he could be so much more. He had not even finished high school and here I had two Masters. In fact my goal was to have been a major political player wherever I lived by the time I was thirty. Instead I was married to a man who acted as if he didn't want to do anything more in life than be a contractor and work for other people. On top of that, when I got home from work I had to make sure that our children had been fed, homework completed, and bathed. Why did I have to do everything? Why couldn't my husband help? He could at least keep the house clean and cook dinner.

My husband jumped in at that point and stated that he tried to do things at home, but that I always found fault with whatever he did, so he just stopped. The therapist then stopped us and showed us the circular cycle that we were doing as a couple. I would fuss and nag my husband repeatedly about any and everything and he in turn would become so angry he would hit me to shut me up and of course I just screamed louder. He would beat me until I was too hurt to talk anymore. She showed us how both of our behaviors were maintaining the problem.

She then asked me something that I thought was outrageous. The therapist asked me why had I married a man that was clearly so far apart from me academically and socially. I had informed her that I was at a fundraiser for several large corporations and businesses and had to attend several functions of this sort. When we were initially married, my husband went to most of the functions with me. Now, he won't go to anything with me. He stated that he didn't go anywhere with me anymore because he felt as though he didn't fit in with "those folks." I told him he could fit in if he would get his GED and then he could start taking some college courses. My husband looked at me and said that that was the problem.

"She wants me to change so I can fit in with her friends." I became quiet and thought about what the therapist had asked me earlier, about our vast differences and our expectations. I loved him, wasn't that enough?

The therapist also pointed out that if I was so successful in my career and in most things that I undertook and he wasn't, then where did that place him in our relationship? Although in no way did she condone abuse of any type, she forced me to look at how my husband might be viewing himself in relationship to me. It was not a pretty picture.

She asked me about my other relationships with other men prior to my marriage. After talking about these relationships, I realized that in those relationships I was always the one who appeared to be the one on top or the one with the most in the relationship. My therapist then related a conversation she had had with someone where the woman insisted that she had to always be right, then her husband must always be wrong. She said that the woman looked shocked and exclaimed that it was not her intention to belittle her husband or to make him feel less than or inferior to her.

The therapist then asked me to consider my motivations for marrying my husband. She asked me if it was possible that I saw myself as a "savior," or rescuer in the relationship with my husband. Pondering on this, I had to take inventory within myself and ask myself was my primary objective with my husband to fix him up to my standards of achievement. My husband was also asked why was he attracted to me, seeing that we were so very different. He stated that he admired very independent women and he related how his mother was also very well educated and very independent. He shared that his mother was the primary breadwinner in their household when they were growing up. My husband also informed us that the only way he knew how to handle any type of disagreement was through fighting, because that was what he saw his father do when he got into an argument with his mother. This was enlightening to me because we did not live in the area with my husband's family and he talked very little about them.

The therapist then showed us how my husband was following the pattern that had been set before him by his father on how to deal with conflict. Talk about seeing things differently, I left that session with an array of thoughts swirling around in my head. Could my perception of men be that they were not complete or all that they could be, but that they needed me to fix them, change them, or perhaps make them better? I decided, sometime later, that I needed some individual therapy as well as marriage therapy.

Twelve

My husband and I are in therapy because he had an affair and I want to know why. We both love each other dearly. In fact, even as we are sitting here we're holding hands, although I am crying. I just don't know how this happened. What was wrong with me? Why did he need another woman? To top all of that off, he also gave me a venereal disease. How can I fix this? What did I do wrong? Those are my questions to the therapist.

I gave her the history of our marriage. We have been married for forty years; we're both in our sixties. For most of the years of our marriage, my husband was a substance abuser. This was nothing new for me because my father was a substance abuser. So, I was used to being in a relationship with a substance abuser. I told the therapist how hard I had prayed to God for Him to stop my husband from abusing substances and abusing drugs. God did answer my prayer and my husband has been clean for almost seventeen years.

What is amazing to me is that he had the affair when he was sober. I feel that I have suffered enough. Why do I still have to feel hurt like this in my life? Every time I think about what my husband has done to me I just cry and cry. I want to stop crying. I feel as though I will always have to face the affair because if he hadn't had the affair then he wouldn't have given me this disease. So, it will always be in my face. I don't know if I can cope with that. My husband states that he wants us to get past this and be a loving couple. With tears in his eyes, he tells the therapist and me how sorry he is and that he has completely severed that relationship with the other woman. But I can't seem to let go of it.

The therapist helped us to work through all of our emotions and our emotional baggage. The crux of the therapy for me was when she showed me how I never got the opportunity to grow as an individual woman, because I was too busy taking care of substance abused men, first my father, then my husband. She helped me to see how I had literally lost myself in their lives, which meant I didn't have a life outside of theirs. When she asked what were my likes and dislikes, hobbies and interests, I had not a clue. Now that I no longer had something to fix or work on, I felt lost.

My husband, for the first time in his life, was finding out who he really was and what he needed in a relationship. We had always had a problem communicating with each other and now that he was clean, it was worse. For thirty years we didn't have to talk to each other. I made all of the important decisions needed regarding our finances, our living conditions, the raising of our children, etc. Being substance free and the man of the house, my husband was now having input into the decision-making process. That was frightening for me. What was I supposed to do? I no longer knew my role in our relationship. I didn't know what to do with my man or how I was supposed to act with him.

Thirteen

I am a forty-three-year-old professional woman and I have AIDS. I am in the health care field, so how could I have gotten AIDS? It was recommended to me to seek therapy by my mother, whom I live with. Since the age of sixteen, I have had multiple sex partners, but I tried to practice safe sex. I always made my partner wear a condom, so I don't know how this could have happened to me. Although my mother is supportive of me, she is also furious with me. I am also very angry with her because I know that she is really more worried about her reputation than she is about me. It has always been that way between us. I remember when I was fourteen and I told her that my stepfather was trying to touch me inappropriately; she slapped me and told me that I was lying. She said that she knew her husband would not do anything that was wrong. I was so upset that she wouldn't believe me and that she chose him over me.

My mother questioned my stepfather about what I had said and he concurred with her that I was lying. A few weeks after that my mother told me that it would be better for everyone if I went and stayed with my aunt, who was her sister. So I had to move from the house that I had lived in all my life. That was tough, but I did it because I figured that in four more years I would be grown and could get my own apartment. I never came back home until now. I only came home because I got sick and couldn't work anymore.

I hate being here. Thinking back on my mom and her relationships with her boyfriends and her husband, it seemed to me as though she always chose them instead of me. I always felt left out. I wonder if my real dad had lived with us, would he have chosen me. Now that I have this disease, I will never have anyone.

Fourteen

Why couldn't mom and dad have let me use their car? If they had let me use the car, then I wouldn't have had to steal it to visit my friends. They are so strict with me. I am tired of living here. I wish I could live somewhere else. Mom and Dad made me come to therapy. There is nothing wrong with me, but there is something wrong with them. They won't let me have any privileges and I am sixteen years old. I am listening to her tell the therapist that I was a perfect or model child until I turned thirteen, and that's when everything changed. She said that she doesn't know what to do with me and dad nods his head in agreement. I wish they all would just leave me alone.

The therapist asked me what was going on and I told her nothing. After some probing from the therapist, I did tell her that if I lived with my real mom and dad then things would definitely be different. She looked a little confused and my mom had to explain to her that they were not my real parents, but in reality they were actually my grandparents. A light seemed to dawn in the therapist's eyes as if she then understood what was going on. I told her that when I was three years old I witnessed my biological father shoot and kill my biological mother. They were both crack addicts. My real father is currently incarcerated serving a life sentence for killing my mother. He shot her eight times. My grandparents adopted me at the age of three, right after it happened. I do love my grandparents and I am glad they adopted me. I even call them mom and dad, but I want to get to know my real family.

My father has been incarcerated most of my life and I want to see him. My parents don't think it would be good for me to visit him in prison. What do they know? After all he is my father. I don't know who I really am or why I act certain ways. Sometimes I get so angry. I think that one day I'm going to get so angry that I'm going to kill someone to, because I do have my dad's genes and I might do like he did to my mother. I fantasize a lot of how it would be if my real mother was living. I am positive she would let me do almost anything I wanted to do. It would be so different from the way it is now. Although I am related to my grandparents, I still don't feel as though I belong.

Fifteen

This is my third husband and I don't know if this marriage is going to work. We have only been married for three years and he has threatened to leave four times. At one time he went so far as to pack his clothes, but in the end he decided to stay. Maybe it would have been better if he had just left then. We seldom talk to each other unless we're conversing about our children. My husband is not their biological father, but he does seem to love them and for the most part he is a good father. I feel so depressed most of the time that the thought of suicide is often a thread that is woven throughout my mind. I try hard not to think about killing myself, because I know I need to live, if not for myself, then for my children. I love my babies.

As I said previously, this is my third marriage. My first husband blackmailed me into marrying him. He threatened to expose a family secret that would have destroyed my family. Not only my personal family, but also my church family would have been devastated. We stayed married for only eighteen months and after him holding a gun to my head and threatening to kill me, I divorced him and hurriedly left that abusive situation. My first child was born prior to me marrying him and he was not his biological father. I was not going to subject him to seeing me be abused by this man. Thus this was the demise of my first marriage.

After being single for about one year, I decided to marry a longtime friend, confidant, and one of the best jazz musicians that I had ever known. By me being a singer and creative person, I felt that we had a lot in common and he seemed to understand me. He did have a history of drug abuse and I had also heard that he had been a drug distributor. I reckoned that I somehow dismissed all of that and was going to accept him on face value, disregarding the past. While being incarcerated, he persuaded me to marry him. He seemed so sincere, he had been clean for at least a year, and I felt that this was really the man that God had for me. So, we were married while he was in jail and I became the faithful wife. I cooked for him, visited him, prayed for him, prayed for us, and did all of the things that I thought a wife should do.

After being released from prison, we lived together as a family with him becoming the priest of our household as we embraced our relationship. During this marriage, I became pregnant with my second child. He had accepted my first child as if it was his and he was ecstatic with this pregnancy, because this child would really be his. Having this child was a blessing or so it seemed. Our family seemed to be going along as any other family. We had our ups and downs but we muddled through.

My husband began to appear restless a few months after our second child was born. I noticed that he was staying away from home more and in conversation he became very abrupt. I tried not to make any waves, but it seemed as though everything I did was wrong. He began to stay away for days on end and dared me to question him. I also began seeing drugs and drug paraphernalia in our bedroom and bathroom. This was frightening to me and I didn't know what to do, so I prayed. I asked God to please stop my husband from selling and using drugs, but it only got worse. I knew I had to leave when he came home one night high out of his mind and raped me.

When he came down from his high, we got into such an ugly fight that I grabbed a butcher knife from the kitchen and tried to kill him. The scary thing about that fight was not that I tried to kill him, but that I wanted to kill him. If I had been the stronger person at that time, I would be in jail today, because I would have killed him. My kids and I left the very next day.

After talking at length with my father, whom I adored, I vowed not to get married again. I would just work and raise my children. Well, life is unpredictable; it never seems to go the way we plan for it to go. I was very much involved in my church when I met my third husband to be. He was a preacher like my father, so I thought surely this would work. At his insistence, after a whirlwind courtship of six months, we were married.

The first few months were great, then we began to see our differences and I could tell that my third husband was not too enthused with who was emerging as his wife. I began to realize that he wanted an old-fashioned traditional wife and I was far from being or becoming that sort of woman. Thus the dirt hit the fan and it has been a downhill slide ever since.

I asked if we could get marriage counseling, but he was not willing to go. What good is it for me to go by myself, if he's not willing to work on our marriage with me? I do have a friend that I talk to that's like an older sister to me. She suggested that I look at my relationship that I had with my father and try to unravel how that relationship was and than compare it to the relationships I had with men throughout my life.

With her help we did just that and I discovered that although I adored my father, I always felt as though he did not approve of me and I was always seeking his approval. My father was the pastor of a significantly large church, had ten children of which I was the youngest. Looking back on my relationship with my father and how I perceived him was an enlightening experience for me. Having to cope with a large and growing church left very little time for my father to spend quality time with his family.

My siblings seemed to be okay with daddy not being around much, but they were much older than I was. There was a ten-year span between my next oldest sibling, and me so I grew up almost like an only child. I don't think my parents had planned on having any other children and I was their surprise baby. I craved my father's attention, but he was just too busy to give me quality time. Sometimes I think he even forgot I was a member of his family, by the way he would look at me. Even now as I think back to how it was growing up, I realize that my father was relatively older when I was born. He was sixty at the time of my birth, so I'm sure he was just plain tired of raising kids. While growing up, my father became an overseer of several churches, thus he had even less time for me.

I tried to be helpful in every possible way, but we never seemed to be able to get our relationship going in the right direction. I tried so hard to please him, but he appeared to take me as a joke as did everyone else in my family. As my friend and I traveled through the men in my life, I began to see how I was still trying to get approval from whichever man was significant in my life at any given time. I was doing this by trying to be whatever they wanted me to be and not being true to my own identity, whatever that was.

I am not quite sure who I am and almost feel schizophrenic trying to be one way for one person and another way for someone else.

Epilogue

Daddy's little girls are all grown up, chronologically, but deep down inside, psychologically, mentally, and emotionally, we still yearn to be "Daddy's Little Girl." We have never filled those lovelorn empty spaces. Thus we search. We search for daddy's love through all of our significant male relationships. Do we know that we are searching to be "Daddy's Little Girl?" I venture to say that we don't know that that is what we're doing. What we do know is that none of our relationships with men work for us. We tend to come out of the relationship feeling less than what we went in with. The men in our lives either leave us through separation, divorce, death, or other women, or we sabotage the relationship and leave them before they can leave us. Because in our mind they are going to eventually leave, so why don't we just do it to them before they do it to us?

As women, we all have an innate desire to belong, to be a part of, to be whole. So, if we as women have those feelings of emptiness then all of our behaviors, actions and reactions are prodding and pushing us to fill those lonely, empty spaces.

The psychological impact of our search to be "Daddy's Little Girl," to fill up all those hurting places leads us as women into unhealthy relationships. These relationships can be physically, emotionally, mentally, and verbally abusive. And we ask ourselves why does this keep happening to me without realizing that we have some responsibility in whatever situation we find ourselves.

Most of us as women have mixed feelings about ourselves. Sometimes we like ourselves; sometimes we don't. We vacillate between periods of relative contentment and times of dissatisfaction. When we feel good about ourselves, we are happy, relaxed, confident, and alert. When we don't feel good about ourselves, we become anxious, irritable, pressured, feeling blue, and depressed.

One of the most important things we possess is our attitude toward our self-image/self-concept of ourselves. Our self-concept is the primary source of our personal happiness or the lack of it. So, as we were growing up our daddies did not give us what we needed to become that self-fulfilled woman and we find ourselves in relationships that are unhealthy. What happens when we're dragging our luggage and trying to fill those empty places within us is that we look toward others, mostly men, to give us our personal happiness? In doing this we place a burden on them that they are unable to fulfill. What we didn't get from our daddies cannot be gotten from other men.

First of all, they are not our fathers. The role that they take should be the role of a spouse, significant other, male friend, and/or brother. Our role as the counterpart is not to be taken care of, but to be a part of, to be equal, to some degree as an adult in an adult relationship. Instead of looking outward for a man to complete us, let us begin to look inward. Let us look to ourselves for our inner healing.

We do this by first loving ourselves. Before we can love another person in a relationship, we must first love ourselves. Before giving love away, we must personally experience love. Love is a decision. It is an act of will, namely an intention and an action. Love is a circular process that begins with self. After we have extended one's self in an evolving process, then we move to a larger state of being to include someone else. Dr. M. Scott Peck defines self-love with love for the other. "Since I am human and you are human, to love humans means to love myself as well as you." How can we give love to others if we ourselves have no knowledge of love?

According to Bruce Narramore in his book, *You're Someone Special,* he states that, "You can love yourself . . . and overcome depression, you can love yourself . . . and learn to handle anger, you can love yourself . . . and resolve your jealousy, you can love yourself . . . and not feel guilty, you can love yourself . . . and learn to relax, you can love yourself . . . and improve your marriage/relationship, and you can love yourself and grow." The question is, how do we as women love ourselves?

We have made the decision to love ourselves, but we don't know what to do or how to even start this evolutionary journey. We desperately want to feel better about ourselves and be in better relationships. Sometimes the only way to progress forward is to go back initially. The first thing we want to do is to identify our internal and external conflicts, negative behaviors, and dysfunctional patterns. Let's actually go back mentally and/or physically and identify the abandonment, the abuses, the betrayals, the rejections, and any other traumatic events that happened in the early years of our lives. We must identify and examine any recurrent dysfunctional behavior patterns that we did and are still doing as a result of these traumatic events. In this phase we must also identify the addictive and compulsive behaviors we learned in the family we were raised in that continue to be demonstrated in our current relationships.

The next thing we want do on our journey to self-love is to identify any unfinished business from our childhood. We have to learn about healthy relationships, their development needs and stages. We must identify the unmet developmental needs that are causing us issues and problems in our current relationships. After identifying these unmet needs, we must then find appropriate activities necessary to meet these developmental needs.

As women we need to also identify our unhealed narcissistic wounds. The next phase of our journey leads us to expressing our core feelings related to our narcissistic wounds. We have to express those deep inner feelings that we are almost ashamed of and/or afraid to verbalize. In doing this we must find safe, supportive relationships where we can learn to express our feeling effectively. We must develop effective self-protective and self-nurturance skills.

Validation from either family members or persons we were raised with about our childhood experiences and feelings will help us to express those core feelings. In completing our unfinished relationship issues, we should contract with willing family members. This can be done by creating corrective parenting contracts, establishing a therapeutic relationship with a professional in the field of counseling and/or psychology to resolve old conflicts, doing self-nurturing activities consistently, and learn to ask directly for what we want and need from others.

In the fifth stage of our process of self-love, we as women must develop autonomous behaviors. By doing this we will set limits and develop healthy boundaries for ourselves without shame or the use of violence. We will confront and change any self-limiting rules and beliefs. It is mandatory that we develop mastery in the areas of self-nurturing and self-care. We must take better care of ourselves and become personally responsible for our own happiness and well-being. As we travel in this stage we have to learn how to resolve conflicts from a win-win position and stop perceiving ourselves as the victim.

The next phase of our journey to wholeness through self-love is focused on our physical well-being. By eating foods that will provide good nutritional support for our bodies, exercising regularly, and getting structural bodywork to break through any emotional patterns stored in our bodies, we will begin a program of effective physical care for us.

One of the most essential, but probably most neglected areas of self-love is the one of spirituality. To become holistic women we must encompass, integrate, and embrace our mind, our body, and our spirit. Through the use of prayer, meditation, retreats, conferences, seminars, workshops, and other spiritual practices we must find our life's purpose and place in the world. Also in taking care of ourselves spiritually, we must forgive our fathers for what they did or did not do for us as their daughters. This forgiveness is not so much for them as it is for us. In order for true healing to take place within us we must let go of the pain, hurt, anger, disappointment, abandonment, and all of the other feelings that we have toward our fathers. This letting go comes through the act of forgiveness. To forgive does not mean for us to forget, but it does mean that we no longer want to punish, hurt, or get even with the individual whom we perceive as the perpetrator of our pain. When we forgive we give up all demand for revenge. This is essential for our healing because when we are in the unforgiving mode, all of our energies are expanded and directed toward the individual(s) who hurt us, in this case our fathers. As we are so focused on extracting payment for what daddy has done to us, either from daddy or from other men in our lives, we are unable to pursue our own individual purpose in life. In essence we've given our power to someone else.

The process of forgiveness is not an easy one and can be quite painful. But if our goal is to seek a higher level of consciousness spiritually, then we cannot avoid pain and suffering. Although we might suffer through the process of forgiveness, ultimately we reap the benefits of a stronger, more complete, self-loved individual. Service to others also helps us to fulfill our purpose. Now that we have followed the path to self-love, we can begin to create partnership relationships based on the principles of co-creation, flexibility, intimacy, and partnership. In these relationships and support systems we can unfold to our highest potential.

For daddy:

Although this book deals specifically with women, we cannot have the woman without the man. Our fathers have a most profound impact on us as we grow into womanhood. The men in our early lives help us to establish the male selection patterns for our future male relationships. So, there are some things men need to understand about the effect they have on us, both positively and negatively, and changes they can make within their behavior that will possibly enhance our relationships with them.

It is very obvious that men and women are clearly different. We think, react, and behave differently. We are supposed to be different. As little girls growing up we observe how daddy treats mommy and we receive certain messages from those interactions and interpret those messages in our finite childish minds as to how we should act in similar situations. Unconsciously we pack that information away into our trunk for future use.

For example, if daddy always speaks in a loud tone to mommy and mommy quietly responds or perhaps says nothing, but immediately does his bidding, we might interpret that behavior as; when daddy yells, mommy does not yell back and/or mommy does what she's supposed to do. So, as a little girl I file into my memory that I should be passive with men, or I should try to have things done or do things that won't make daddy or any man speak harshly to me.

The little girl in me can also interpret that scenario by becoming defensive and decide that no man will ever speak to me in that tone of voice, thus I become very strong and independent and carry the facade that dares any man to cross. This maladaptive behavior can be a result of a little's girl's interpretation of her experience.

So, one of the things men should know is to be cautious or take note on how they communicate with their spouse, their partner, their significant other, especially if a little girl is involved in the relationship, be it a daughter, a sister, a friend, etc. Not only is communication important, but also how the man treats the woman in his life in general, is also another way in which girls tend to look at and interpret behavior in that relationship. From that relationship, they perceive what they want in their future relationship with a man.

Predicated upon what they see in the male/female relationship(s) as they grow up, girls will make choices and/or preferences about what they will and will not have or tolerate in their future relationships. They also become observant of what motivates the man. They are constantly trying to find out what makes daddy tick. Little girls want to know what makes their daddy happy, sad, angry, disappointed, and all of the other feelings that daddy expresses. She not only wants to know what motivates daddy, but she will try and fix things, if she perceives that her counterpart, mommy or the significant female in the relationship, is not holding up to her end of the bargain, from her observations. The little girl needs to see her daddy, or that significant man in her life, caring for her mommy. The man can show that he cares by showing interest in the woman's feelings, concern for her well-being, and by making her feel special.

The man to the little girl, usually from a father to a daughter, should also demonstrate this caring feeling. Daddy needs to learn to listen without judgment, but with empathy and relatedness to a woman, or girl as she expresses her feelings. He does not have to try and solve and/or fix everything. Daddy in his understanding attitude does not presume to already know the thoughts or feelings that he hears, but rather gathers meaning from what is heard and validates what is being communicated. Daddy needs to respond to a woman in such a way that she feels respected, because he has made her rights, needs, and wishes a priority.

A spouse, girlfriend, daughter, or significant other also needs to feel adored and special. A man fulfills this need when he makes the feelings and needs of the woman or girl more important than his other interests like work, leisure time, study, etc. A woman or girl feels validated when the man does not object to or argue with her about her feelings and wants, but instead accepts and confirms those feelings. When a man, be it father, daddy, boyfriend, brother, etc. consistently demonstrates that he cares, respects, understands, validates, and is devoted to the woman and /or girl in his life, then she feels secure and loved in that relationship.

If daddy's little girl sees a healthy male/female relationship as she grows up, then she will have a better chance of being in healthy relationships with men and an even better chance at a surviving healthy marriage if she so chooses. The same is true if she grows up viewing unhealthy male/female relationships.

So, dads, let it be known that you help us in deciding what we pack as we fill our trunks for our journey through life. For what you give of yourself passes on through us. We are Daddy's Little Girl.

As quoted by Kahlil Gibran from *The Prophet*:

Your children are not your children.
They are the sons and daughters of Life's longing for itself.
They come through you but not from you,
And though they are with you
yet they do not belong to you.
You may give them your love but not your thoughts,
For they have their own thoughts.

You may house their bodies but not their souls,
For their souls dwell in the house of tomorrow, which you
cannot visit,
not even in your dreams.
You may strive to be like them,
but seek not to make them like you,
For life goes not backward nor tarries with yesterday.
You are the bows from which your children as living arrows
are sent forth.
The archer sees the mark upon the path of the infinite,
and He bends you with His might
that his arrows may go swift and far.
Let your bending in the archer's hand be for gladness;
For even as He loves the arrow that flies,
so He loves also the bow that is stable.

Bibliography

Adler, A. (1952). *The Practice and Theory of Individual Psychology.* New York: Humanities Press.

Ainsworth, M. & Eichberg, C. (1991). Effects of mother's unresolved loss of an attachment figure. In C. Parkes, J. Hinde, & P. Marris (Eds.), Attachment Across the Life Cycle (pp. 160–183). NY: Routledge.

Almeida, D. & Galambos, N. (1993). Continuity and change in father-adolescent relations. In S. Shulman & A. Collins (Eds.), Father-adolescent Relations (San Francisco: Jossey Bass).

Ambert, A. (1996). *The Effects of Children on Parents.* NY: Haworth.

Appleton, W. (1981). *Fathers and Daughters.* NY: Berkeley Books.

Barras, J. (2000). *Whatever Happened to Daddy's Little Girl?* Miami: One World Press.

Belsky, J. (1998). Paternal influence and children's well-being. In A. Booth & A. Crouter (Eds.), *Men in Families.* Mahway, NJ: Erlbaum.

Berry, C. & Barrington, L. (1998). *Daddies and Daughters.* NY: Scribner.

Biller, H. (1993). *Fathers and Families: Paternal factors in child development.* Westport, CT: Auburn House.

Blankenhorn, D. (1994). *Fatherless America.* NY: Basic Books.

Booth, A. (1998). *Men in Families.* Mahway, NJ: Erlbaum.

Bowen, M. (1961). Family psychotherapy. *American Journal of Orthopsychiatry,* 31. (40–60).

Bronstein, P. (1999). Differences in mothers' & fathers' behaviors toward children. In L. Peplau & S. DeBro (Eds.), *Gender, Cultures and Ethnicity* (Mountain View, CA: Mayfield Press).

Carr, A. (1998). Including fathers in family therapy. Contemporary Family Therapy, 20. (371–383).

Cochran, D. (2000). African American father-daughter relationships. DC: National Institutes of Health.

Coley, R. & Chase, L. (1999). Stability and change in involvement among African American fathers. *Journal of Family Psychology*, 13. (416--435).

Cook, M. & Styron, W. (1994). *Fathers and Daughters: In their own words*. NY: Chronicle Books.

Cummings, M. & O'Reily, A. (1997). Effects of marital quality on child adjustment. ln M. Lamb (Ed.), The role of the father in child development (pp.49–65). NY: Wiley.

Daniels, C. (1998). *Lost Fathers*. NY: St. Martins Press.

Declaire, J., Gottman, J., & Goleman, D. (2000). *Raising an Emotionally Intelligent Child*. NY: Fireside.

Dicks, H. V. (1963). Object relations theory and marital studies. British Journal of Medical Psychology, 36. (125–129).

Early, G. (1994). *Daughters: On family and fatherhood*. Reading, PA: Addison Wesley.

Erickson, B. (1998). *Longing for Dad: Father loss and its impact*. Deerfield Beach, FL: Health Communications.

Feldman, L. (1990). Fathers and fathering. ln R. Meth & R. Pasick (Eds.), *Men in Therapy* (pp. 88–107). NY: Guilford.

Fenell, D.L. & Weinhold, B.K. (1997). *Counseling Families: An Introduction to Marriage and Family Therapy*. Denver: Love Publishing Company.

Gibran, Kahlil (1923). *The Prophet*. New York: Alfred A. Knopf, Inc.

Goetz, M. (1999). *My Father, Myself: A guide to reconciliation for sons and daughters*. Boston, Mass: Element.

Gordon, B. (1996). *Your father, Yourself*. NY: Birch Lane. Gottlieb, D. (1991). *Voices in the family: Healing in the heart of the family*. NY: Signet.

Gottman, J. (1998). A model of men in marriages and families. ln A. Booth & A. Crouter (Eds.), *Men in Families* (pp. 149–192). Mahweh, NJ: Erlbaum.

Goulter, B. & Minninger, J. (1993). *The Father Daughter Dance.* NY: Putnam.

Greer, G. (1990). *Daddy, We Hardly Knew You.* NY: Knopf.

Greif, G. (1997). *Out of Touch.* Cambridge, MA: Oxford University.

Griswold, R. (1998). History and politics of fatherlessness. In C. Daniels (Ed.), *Lost Fathers.* NY: St. Martin's.

Hamer, J. (2000). The definition of fatherhood for never married African Americans. *Journal of Sociology & Social Welfare, 25,* 81–104.

Harris, M. (1996). *The Loss that is Forever: Impact of the early death of a mother or father.* NY: Plume.

Hazard, D. & Farris, M. (1996) *How a Man Prepares His Daughters for Life.* Bethany House.

Henry, D. & McPherson, J. (1998). *Fathering Daughters: Reflections by men.* Boston, Mass.: Beacon.

Hetherington, E. M. (1972). Effects of father absence on personality development in adolescent daughters. Developmental Psychology 7. (3) (313–326).

Hosley, C. & Montemayor, R. (1997). Fathers and adolescents. In M. Lamb (Ed.), *The Role of the Father in Child Development* (pp. 162–178). NY: Wiley.

Hutchinson, E. (1995). *Black Fatherhood: The guide to male parenting.* Boston, MA: Impact Press.

Kast, V. (1997). *Father-Daughter, Mother-Son.* Rockport, Mass: Element.

Lamb, M. (1997). *The Role of the Father in Child Development.* NY: Wiley.

Larson, W. (1993). Finding time for fatherhood: Adolescent-father interactions. In S. Shulman & A. Collins (Eds.), *Father-Adolescent Relations.* San Francisco: Jossey Bass.

Leaper, C., Anderson, K., & Sanders, P. (1998). Gender effects on parents' talk to their children. Developmental Psychology, 34, 3–27.

Leman, K. (2000). *What a Difference Daddy Makes.* Thomas Nelson.

Leonard, L. (1998). *The Wounded Woman: Healing the father daughter wound.* Boston, Mass.: Shambala.

Levine, R. & Pitinsky, T. (1998). *Working Fathers: Strategies for balancing work and family.* Reading, Mass.: Addison Wesley.
Levine, S. (2000). *Father Courage: what happens when men put family first.* NY: Harcourt.
Long, D. (2000). *He's Just My Dad.* NY: Harper.
Long, N. (1997). Are we contributing to the devaluation of fathers? Clinical ChiM Psychology & Psychiatry, 2, 197–200.
Loomis, M. (1995). *Her Father's Daughter.* Wilmetre, IL: Chiron Press.
Loritts, C. (1998). *Never Walk Away: Lesson from a father who lived it.* Moody Press.
Lyons, S. (1996). *Landscape of the Heart: Writings on daughters and journeys.* Seattle, Wash.: Washington State University.
Marone, N. (1998). *How to Father a Successful Daughter.* NY: Fawcett.
Morgan, J. & Wilcoxon, A. (1998). Fathers and daughters: Recognizing the significance. Family Therapy, 25, 73–84.
Munsch, J., Woodward, J., & Darling, N. (1995). Children's perceptions of their relationships with coresiding and non-coresiding fathers. *Journal of Divorce & Remarriage,* 23, 39–55. Murdock, M. (1996). *Fathers' Daughters.* NY: Fawcett.
Owen, U. (1985) *Fathers: Reflections by Daughters.* NY: Pantheon.
Peck, S. M. (1978). *The Road Less Traveled.* NY: Simon & Schuster. A Touchstone Book.
Peterson, D. & Kilpatrick, S. (1999). Fathers & Daughters, *Psychology Today,* December.
Phares, V. (1999). *Poppa Psychology: The role of fathers in children's mental well-being.* Westport, CT: Praegar.
Pipher, M. (1994). *Reviving Ophelia.* NY: Putnam.
Pittman, F. (1999). *Grow up! How Taking Responsibility Can Make You a Happy Adult.* NY: Golden Books.
Pleck, E.& Pleck, J. (1997). Fatherhood ideals in the U.S. In M.Lamb (Ed.), *The Role of the Father in Child Development* (pp. 33-48). NY: Wiley.
Popenoe, D. (1996). *Life Without Father.* N: Simon & Schuster.
Rogers, C. (1961). *On Becoming a Person.* Boston: Houghton Mifflin.

Scull, C. (1992). *Fathers, Sons and Daughters.* Los Angeles, CA: Jeremy Tarcher.
Secunda, V. (1992). *Women and Their Fathers.* NY: Bantam Doubleday Dell.
Secunda, V. (1992). *Women and Their Fathers.* NY: Delacorte Press.
Sharpe, S. (1994). *Fathers and Daughters.* NY: Routledge.
Snarey, J. (1993). *How Fathers Care for the Next Generation.* Cambridge, MA: Harvard University.
Wakerman, E. (1984). *Father Loss: Daughters discuss the man that got away.* NY: Doubleday.
Way, N. & Stauber, H. (1996). Are absent fathers really absent? In B. Leadbeater & N. Way (Ed.), Urban Girls (pp.132–148). NY: New York University.
Wild, J. (2000). *Women, Men & Children Surviving Divorce & Separation.* NY: John Wiley.
Williams, E. & Radin, N. (1999). Effect of father participation in child rearing. *American Journal of Orthopsychiatry,* 69, 328–336.
Wolgemuth, R. (1999). She calls me daddy. Focus on Families. Zipes, J. (1994). *Fairy Tale as Myth: Myth as Fairy Tale.* Louisville: University of Kentucky.